DATE DUE		

COMPREHENSIVE RESEARCH
AND STUDY GUIDE

Maya Angelou

EDITED AND WITH AN INTRODUCTION
BY HAROLD BLOOM

CURRENTLY AVAILABLE

BLOOM'S MAJOR SHORT STORY WRITERS

Sherwood Anderson
Jorge Luis Borges
Italo Calvino
Raymond Carver
Anton Chekhov
Joseph Conrad
Stephen Crane
William Faulkner
F. Scott Fitzgerald
Nathaniel Hawthorne
Ernest Hemingway
O. Henry
Shirley Jackson
Henry James
James Joyce
Franz Kafka
D. H. Lawrence
Jack London
Thomas Mann
Herman Melville
Flannery O'Connor
Edgar Allan Poe
Katherine Anne Porter
J. D. Salinger
John Steinbeck
Mark Twain
John Updike
Eudora Welty

BLOOM'S MAJOR POETS

Maya Angelou
Elizabeth Bishop
William Blake
Gwendolyn Brooks
Robert Browning
Geoffrey Chaucer
Samuel T. Coleridge
Dante
Emily Dickinson
John Donne
Hilda Doolittle (H.D.)
T. S. Eliot
Robert Frost
Seamus Heaney
Homer
Langston Hughes
John Keats
John Milton
Sylvia Plath
Edgar Allan Poe
Poets of World War I
Shakespeare's Poems & Sonnets
Percy Shelley
Alfred, Lord Tennyson
Walt Whitman
William Carlos Williams
William Wordsworth
William Butler Yeats

Maya Angelou

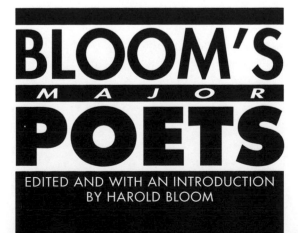

BLOOM'S *MAJOR* POETS

EDITED AND WITH AN INTRODUCTION
BY HAROLD BLOOM

© 2001 by Chelsea House Publishers,
a subsidiary of Haights Cross Communications.

Introduction © 2001 by Harold Bloom.

Printed and bound in the United States of America.

3 5 7 9 8 6 4 2

Library of Congress Cataloging-in-Publication Data

Maya Angelou / Harold Bloom, editor.
    p. cm. – (Bloom's major poets)
  Includes bibliographical references and index.
  ISBN 0-7910-5937-5 (alk. paper)
    1. Angelou, Maya—Criticism and interpretation—Handbooks,
manuals, etc. 2. Women and literature—United States—History—20th
Century—Handbooks, manuals, etc. 3. African American women in
literature—Handbooks, manuals, etc. 4. African Americans in
literature—Handbooks, manuals, etc. I. Bloom, Harold. II. Series.

  PS3551.N464 Z763 2001
  818'.5409—dc21

                    2001028514

Chelsea House Publishers
1974 Sproul Road, Suite 400
Broomall, PA 19008-0914

www.chelseahouse.com

Contributing Editor: Mirjana Kalezic

Produced for Chelsea House Publishers by:
Robert Gerson Publisher's Services, Santa Barbara, CA

Contents

User's Guide

This volume is designed to present biographical, critical, and bibliographical information on the author's best-known or most important poems. Following Harold Bloom's editor's note and introduction is a detailed biography of the author, discussing major life events and important literary accomplishments. A thematic and structural analysis of each poem follows, tracing significant themes, patterns, and motifs in the work.

A selection of critical extracts, derived from previously published material from leading critics, analyzes aspects of each poem. The extracts consist of statements from the author, if available, early reviews of the work, and later evaluations up to the present. A bibliography of the author's writings (including a complete list of all books written, cowritten, edited, and translated), a list of additional books and articles on the author and the work, and an index of themes and ideas in the author's writings conclude the volume.

~

Harold Bloom is Sterling Professor of the Humanities at Yale University and Henry W. and Albert A. Berg Professor of English at the New York University Graduate School. He is the author of over 20 books, including *Shelley's Mythmaking* (1959), *The Visionary Company* (1961), *Blake's Apocalypse* (1963), *Yeats* (1970), *A Map of Misreading* (1975), *Kabbalah and Criticism* (1975), *Agon: Toward a Theory of Revisionism* (1982), *The American Religion* (1992), *The Western Canon* (1994), and *Omens of Millennium: The Gnosis of Angels, Dreams, and Resurrection* (1996). *The Anxiety of Influence* (1973) sets forth Professor Bloom's provocative theory of the literary relationships between the great writers and their predecessors. His most recent books include *Shakespeare: The Invention of the Human*, a 1998 National Book Award finalist, and *How to Read and Why*, which was published in 2000.

Professor Bloom earned his Ph.D. from Yale University in 1955 and has served on the Yale faculty since then. He is a 1985 MacArthur Foundation Award recipient, served as the Charles Eliot Norton Professor of Poetry at Harvard University in 1987–88, and has received honorary degrees from the universities of Rome and Bologna. In 1999, Professor Bloom received the prestigious American Academy of Arts and Letters Gold Medal for Criticism.

Currently, Harold Bloom is the editor of numerous Chelsea House volumes of literary criticism, including the series BLOOM'S NOTES, BLOOM'S MAJOR DRAMATISTS, BLOOM'S MAJOR NOVELISTS, MAJOR LITERARY CHARACTERS, MODERN CRITICAL VIEWS, MODERN CRITICAL INTERPRETATIONS, and WOMEN WRITERS OF ENGLISH AND THEIR WORKS.

Editor's Note

My Introduction briefly indicates why Angelou, as a writer of "popular poetry," is largely exempt from criticism.

Among the large numbers of reviews and critical extracts, I find particularly interesting those by James Finn Cotter, Lynn Z. Bloom, May Jane Lupton, and Robert B. Stepto.

Introduction

HAROLD BLOOM

Maya Angelou is best known for the initial volume, *I Know Why the Caged Bird Sings,* of her still-ongoing autobiography. Her poetry has a large public, but very little critical esteem. It is, in every sense, "popular poetry," and makes no formal or cognitive demands upon the reader.

Of Angelou's sincerity, good-will towards all, and personal vitality, there can be no doubt. She is professedly an inspirational writer, of the self-help variety, which perhaps places her beyond criticism.

Her lyric cadences, to my ear, have little resemblance to the blues, and seem closer to country-music. Angelou's most persuasive defender is the scholar-critic, Robert B. Stepto, who carefully distinguishes her use of folk idioms and forms from her weaker work. Stepto essentially asks us to yield to Angelou's self-presentation, and thus to import the autobiographical volumes back into the weaker poems.

Angelou seems best at ballads, the most traditional kind of popular poetry. The function of such work is necessarily social rather than aesthetic, particularly in an era totally dominated by visual media. One has to be grateful for the benignity, humor, and wholeheartedness of Angelou's project, even if her autobiographical prose necessarily centers her achievement. ❀

Biography of
Maya Angelou

Maya Angelou is a writer, poet, actress, playwright, civil rights activist, film producer, and director. She lectures throughout the United States and abroad. She has published 10 best-selling books and countless magazine articles.

She was born Marguerite Johnson on April 4, 1928, in St. Louis, to Bailey and Vivian Baxter Johnson. Her brother Bailey gave her the name Maya. When she was three and a half year old, her parents divorced and sent her and her brother to Stamps, Arkansas, to live with their paternal grandmother, Annie Henderson.

Maya Angelou describes vividly the desolate journey from California to Arkansas in the autobiography that has since brought her fame, *I Know Why the Caged Bird Sings,* published when she was 41. The book covers her life from childhood and describes the way she was raised in segregated rural Arkansas, until the birth of her son at the age of 17. Her other four subsequent prose books continue her life story, proceeding chronologically. In *Gather Together in My Name* (1974) she depicts her life as a teenage mother, her introduction to drugs and illicit activities, and the hardship of bare economic survival. Her young adult years as a show-business personality provide the content for *Singin' and Swingin' and Gettin' Merry Like Christmas* (1976); her life as a racial and social activist is covered in *The Heart of a Woman* (1981); and the final autobiography, *All God's Children Need Traveling Shoes* (1986), explores her African journey from 1962 until 1965.

After graduating from Lafayette County training school in Arkansas, Maya Angelou, along with her brother, moved to San Francisco, where she attended high school. She received a two-year scholarship to study dance and drama at the California Labor School, but in 1944, she became pregnant and gave birth to a son. In her late teens she supported herself as a Creole-style cook, nightclub waitress, and a streetcar conductor.

In the early '50s, she married Tosh Angelos. (Her last name is a variation of her then husband's last name.) Angelos was a Greek sailor whom she met when she worked in a record store in San Francisco.

Sometime during those years, she found her way into a job as a dancer and singer. She had a winning way with audiences, and she performed in the popular West Indian Calypso style at the Purple Onion, a cabaret in San Francisco. She also appeared in the role of Ruby in *Porgy and Bess,* a U.S. Department of State–sponsored musical that toured 22 nations in Europe. She studied with Martha Graham, and, as she describes in her collection of personal essays, *Wouldn't Take Nothing for My Journey Now* (1993), she had a dancing partnership with Alvin Ailey (1933–1989) for the Al and Rita Show.

In the late '50s, after divorcing Tosh, she moved to New York City and became involved in the political and literary scene there. But her career as an actress continued to grow; it reached its high point in 1960 when she acted the White Queen in Jean Genet's satirical play, *The Blacks.* She was also the most politically active in this period of her life: she organized a fund-raiser called "Cabaret for Freedom" in support of Martin Luther King Jr. As a result of this, she was appointed Northern Coordinator of the Southern Christian Leadership Conference (SCLC), a position she held briefly from 1959 to 1960.

In 1961, she fell in love with a South African dissident lawyer, Vusumzi Muke, and moved to Cairo with him. There, she worked as associate editor of *The Arab Observer,* the only English-language news weekly in the Middle East, and as assistant administrator of the School of Music and Drama with the University of Ghana.

As she depicts in *All God's Children Need Traveling Shoes,* during her time in Africa she met several people who affected her life and character. One of them was Julian Mayfield, the renowned scholar of W.E.B. Du Bois, and the other one was black Muslim Leader El-Hajj Malik El-Shabazz, known as Malcolm X.

Two horrifying events deeply influenced Maya Angelou on her return to the United States. The first was the assassination of Malcom X on February 21, 1965, and the other was the killing of Martin Luther King in 1968.

In 1971, she published a volume of poetry, *Just Give Me a Cool Drink of Water 'Fore I Diiie,* which was nominated for a Pulitzer Prize.

Her marriage, to Paul Du Feu, took place in 1973 (and ended in divorce in 1980). In 1975, President Ford appointed her to the American Revolution Council. Another book of poetry, *And Still I*

Rise, was published in 1978. The next collection of poems *I Shall Not Be Moved* didn't appear till 1990.

In the last three decades she has written and produced several prize-winning documentaries, including *Afro-Americans in the Arts,* a PBS special for which she received the Golden Eagle, and *Black, Blues, Black,* a 10-part program about the prominent role of African culture in American life. With *Georgia, Georgia,* she became the first black woman to have a screenplay produced. She also wrote the script and musical score for the television version of *I Know Why the Caged Bird Sings.* Along with all this she has made hundreds of stage and television appearances.

In 1993, at the request of President Clinton, she delivered the poem "On the Pulse of Morning" at his inauguration. This was the first time a poet had taken part in an inauguration since Robert Frost spoke at President Kennedy's. The same year, she published *Wouldn't Take Nothing for My Journey Now,* a collection of essays on lessons in living, which, like most of its predecessors, was a best-seller. Prestigious institutions, like Smith College and Mills College, have granted her honorary doctorates; reportedly, she now holds fifty.

She currently resides in Winston-Salem, North Carolina, where she has a lifetime appointment as the first Reynolds Professor and Chair of American Studies at Wake Forest University. ❁

Reviews of
Maya Angelou's Poetry

Just Give Me a Cool Drink of Water 'Fore I Diiie

Angelou's *I Know Why the Caged Bird Sings* was a best seller, and there will be an audience for this rather well done schlock poetry, not to be confused with poetry for people who read poetry. It's like *This Is My Beloved* coupled with black rage, and some of the rhymed lyrics are better than that. Nina Simone might do well to set a few of them to music: the first poem, "They Went Home," isn't one of the best, but it fits into the torchy unrequited love bag: "They went home and told their wives, / that never once in all their lives, / had they known a girl like me. / But . . . They went home." This collection isn't accomplished, not by any means; but some readers are going to love it.

> —John Alfred Avant, review of *Just Give Me a Cool Drink of Water 'Fore I Diiie* by Maya Angelou, *Library Journal* 96 (1971): p. 3329.

This slim volume of marvelously lyrical, rhythmical poems is divided into two sections. Part One contains poetry of love, and therefore of anguish, sharing, fear, affection and loneliness. Part Two features poetry of racial confrontation—of protest, anger and irony. YA's will enjoy this as much as they did the author's *I Know Why the Caged Bird Sings*.

> —Martha Liddy, review of *Just Give Me a Cool Drink of Water 'Fore I Diiie* by Maya Angelou, *Library Journal* 96 (1971): p. 3916.

Thirty-nine lyrics (craftsmanlike and powerful though not great poetry) by a distinguished black artist. The most effective are in the second section, "Just before the world ends"—bitterly angry poems expressing the will to survive of a strong woman "Too proud to bend / Too poor to break." Recommended for any library with an Afro-American collection.

> —Unsigned review in *Choice* 9, no. 2 (April 1972): p. 210.

Angelou's new volume is slim, with good heritage ballads and excellent lyrics such as "Child Dead in Old Seas," and the colorful, pleasant "This Winter Day," which reminds one of genre painting. The poems work best read aloud.

—Kathryn Gibbs Harris, review of *Oh Pray My Wings Are Gonna Fit Me Well* by Maya Angelou, *Library Journal* 100, no. 17 (1975): p. 1829.

The grouping of the 36 poems in *Oh Pray My Wings Are Gonna Fit Me Well* is somewhat distracting but does not diminish the streetwise soundings infused with a particular pride and pain. "Here's to Adhering" is a simple rhyme until its structure slaps you; the sardonic quality of "On Reaching Forty" reduces age to a minor milestone; nationhood is elevated to a higher yet deeper plane in "Africa" and in "America." "The Pusher" is a typical Angelou acceleration, but it is "Chicken-Licken" that causes a dead halt.

—Unsigned review in *Booklist* 72, no. 4 (October 1975): p. 279.

The multi-talented Maya Angelou (producer, director, actress, film writer, author of two outstanding autobiographies) in her second book of poetry writes poems of love, insight, tension, and the black condition celebrated triumphant over difficulties. The poems are uneven, at times banal (e.g. "Greyday": "No one knows / my lonely heart / when we're apart." But the best soar with vivid images such as these from "This winter day": "The kitchen in its readiness / white green and orange things / leak their blood selves in the soup." And lines like those in "Pickin em up and layin em down" beg to be read aloud. Most of these poems are to be reread and laughed over and thought about. Recommended especially for black collections.

—Unsigned review in *Choice* 12, no. 11 (January 1976): p. 1439.

Too much fame too soon has been the ruin of many poets. Until recently, black poets have not had to suffer this dubious blessing. Poets like Robert Hayden won recognition abroad but were ignored by our own literary king-makers. Hayden's collection of new and selected poems in a climate that is more openly aware should bring him the fame his talent deserves, and, luckily, it comes too late to harm that gift.

African roots and personal memories provide the main theme for these poems. A long poem, "Middle Passage," recalls the terrors of the slave route from Africa to the West Indies. The manner is similar to Hart Crane's "The Bridge," but the content is more accessible and dramatic. Hayden is a master of voices used in narrative verse; he makes the slave owner's account of a black mutiny savagely ironic in the conclusion of "Middle Passage." In "The Ballad of Sue Ellen Westerfield" and "Aunt Jemima on the Ocean Waves," he dramatizes the black woman's frustrated loves through the women's own memories. The poet remembers his own father rising early to stoke the fire in the moving poem, "Those Winter Sundays."

The past is remembered and preserved through the poem. One's ancestors live again in lines like these: "Greatgrandma Easter, on my father's side, / was a Virginia freedman's Indian bride. / She was more than six feet tall. At ninety could / still chop and tote firewood." Even the ancient past lives beyond its accidental preservation in museums. Nefertiti and Akhenaten become characters of flesh and bone in another fine poem. In "The Night-Blooming Cereus," the poet describes the mysterious blossoming of an exotic plant indoors and sees in it an action "ancient as prayers invoking Osiris, Krishna, / Tezcatlipoca. / We spoke / in whispers when / we spoke / at all."

Hayden keeps his eyes and ears open to the magic of the moment, to the moose in the wood ("tall ungainly creatures / in their battle crowns") to the "Creole babies, / Dixie odalisques, / speeding through cutglass / dark." A window washer, a religious confidence man, hunters or country dancers play their momentary part in his parody of freak and minstrel shows. Anger and love move these images into being, and, as in all true poetry, language gives them life. Robert Hayden will survive in his poems, long after current fashions of literature fade.

On the other side of the ledger, Nikki Giovanni and Maya Angelou in their latest collections offer unfortunate examples of the dangers of success. Both are self-consciously determined to speak as black women of their African past and of their present loves. Both fail because the public voice drowns out the private emotion. In fairness, Nikki Giovanni retains in some of her new work the innocent clarity that marked her earlier poems. "Kidnap Poem" is a delight: "if I were a poet / I'd kidnap you. . . ." And in "All I Gotta Do," one hears the authentic note of the blues. She sometimes shows an eye for detail, as in "Alabama Poem" when she describes an old woman with a corncob pipe knifing a bunion off her foot. But too often we are assaulted with generalities like: "'life is precious' is all we poets / wrapped in our loneliness are trying to say." Maya Angelou is guilty of worse: "No one knows / my lonely heart / when we're apart."

Too many public readings may prove the undoing of the personal voice. What wows an audience may offend on the printed page. Poets like Hayden need to be read aloud because the voice waits there for us: "Voyage through death / to life upon these shores." They tell us of the journey we all hear in the heart beyond the color of our skin or the applause of the crowd.

—James Finn Cotter, review of *Oh Pray My Wings Are Gonna Fit Me Well* by Maya Angelou, *The Women and The Men* by Nikki Giovanni and *The Peacock Poems* by Shirley Williams, *America* 134, no. 5 (February 1976): pp. 103–4.

And Still I Rise

To her third collection of poems the author has brought a life full of zest and style that is phenomenally her own. Her secret lies, she says lyrically, "in the reach of my arms / The span of my hips, / The stride of my step, / The curl of my lips. / I'm a woman / Phenomenally. / Phenomenal woman, / That's me." She finds rhythm in everything in life. She is not afraid to dream, to love, and to be brazenly, saucily, deeply herself. She writes of her past, of grinning, dancing, colorful city folk and sullen suburbanites, of woman's work, of cotton and sugar cane, and of slaves. She thanks God for letting her live and tells the world, "You may write me down in history / With your bitter, twisted lies, / You may trod me in the very dirt / But still, like dust, I'll rise."

—Mary Silva Cosgrave, review of *And Still I Rise* by Maya Angelou, *Horn Book Magazine* 55, no. 1 (1979): p. 97.

Angelou's new volume of poetry enlarges on themes from her auto-biographical writings and earlier poetry, although the quality of individual poems varies. Some lines jump and dance: "Wino men, old men / Young men sharp as mustard / See them walk, Men are always / Going somewhere." Other poems hobble: "Father, Father / My life give I gladly to thee / Deep rivers ahead / High mountains above / My soul wants only your love." The poems that work have language close to speech or more nearly to song, while the others get mired in hackneyed metaphor and forced rhyme. Despite its unevenness, the book succeeds as a statement of one black woman's experience, and of her determination not only to survive but to grow. For large poetry or black literature collections.

> —Joyce Boyarin Blundell, review of *And Still I Rise* by Maya Angelou, *Library Journal* 103 (1978): p. 1640.

Angelou's new book of poetry begins with a joyful section entitled "Touch Me, Life, Not Softly," which serves as an affirmation of the author's strength as a woman and as a lover. "Phenomenal Woman" celebrates her slightly mysterious power, and "Men" recreates the excitement provoked by *those* mysterious creatures. Part II, "Traveling," details the hardships encountered by the author and/or her people—drug addiction, child abuse, inner-city life, and conditions in the Old South. Angelou injects hope here through humor: "Lady Luncheon Club," for instance, is a tongue-in-cheek description of an overly intellectual speaker at a woman's club. "And Still I Rise," the third section, reiterates the celebration of Part I, as Angelou finds renewed and collective strength. The title poem is a proud, even defiant statement on behalf of all Black people. The book ends with praise and thanks for life, and for God. Many young people will identify with Angelou's descriptions of Black city life and will be cheered by her enthusiasm. However, Angelou is more adept at prose than verse, and the strength here is even more evident in her autobiographical *I Know Why the Caged Bird Sings.*

> —Ellen Lippmann, review of *And Still I Rise* by Maya Angelou, *School Library Journal* 25 (November 1978): p. 108.

Angelou is best known for her penetrating autobiographies: *I Know Why the Caged Bird Sings, Gather Together in My Name,* and *Heart of a Woman.* Unfortunately, this fourth volume of her poetry is no match for her prose writings. The reader is jarred by stilted, "poetic" language and sing-song, school-girlish rhyme. The best poems are those that swing with a touch of the blues, as in "Weekend Glory": My life ain't heaven / but it sure ain't hell. I'm not on top / but I call it swell / if I'm able to work / and get paid right / and have the luck to be Black / on a Saturday night." For collections where there is proven interest.

> —Janet Boyarin Blundell, review of *Shaker, Why Don't You Sing* by Maya Angelou, *Library Journal* 108, no. 7 (1983): pp. 746, 748.

The fourth collection of poetry by the author, a celebrity of many talents, is a lyrical outpouring of seasoned feelings from the heart and mind. Her "Family Affairs" shrewdly encloses centuries of black history in a verse-play on the Rapunzel story; "Caged Bird" is a lament for a freedom never known; "Prescience" brings to mind Robert Burns's eighteenth-century love song of parting; "Amoebaean For Daddy" is a belated plea for forgiveness. Writing of the blues, of recovering from passion, of the smells and sounds of Southern cities, of living life right on Saturday night, Angelou is musical, rhythmical, and enchanting.

> —Mary Silva Cosgrave, review of *Shaker, Why Don't You Sing* by Maya Angelou, *Horn Book Magazine* 59, no. 3 (June 1983): p. 336.

I Shall Not Be Moved

"Big ships shudder, / down to the sea / because of me / Railroads run / on a twinness track / 'cause of my back." In Angelou's exquisitely simple worksong, both wit and longing seem to be rooted in physical action. Like Paul Robeson's singing, like Langston Hughes' "Florida Road Workers," rhythm and sense are one. The other poems in this collection don't come up to "Worker's Song"—some are too polemical—but in the best of them, the sensuous detail livens the abstraction ("Old folks / allow their bellies to jiggle like slow / tambourines . . . / When old folks laugh, they free the world"). There's no false sentiment ("Preacher, don't send me / when I die / to some big ghetto in the sky"); Angelou's paradise has no "grits and tripe"; but "the music is jazz / and the season is fall." The dying fall of many lines combined with the strong beat reinforces the feeling of struggle and uncertainty: "Why do we journey, muttering / like rumors among the stars?"

—Hazel Rochman, review of *I Shall Not Be Moved* by Maya Angelou, *Booklist* 86, no. 18 (May 1990): p. 1773.

Although Angelou addresses the black experience, "because it is the one in which I am most familiar," she draws from different ethnic backgrounds "talking about things relative to the human condition— what human beings can endure, dream, fail at and still survive." ⟨. . .⟩

Asked about the book's title, she said: "I think that a number of people in positions of power have ignored, denied or neglected their positions and ability to change the world. The title reflects an encouraging statement to young people—to have a moral stance and to avoid saying 'I Shall Not Be Moved.'" ⟨. . .⟩

Her newest collection of poetry begins with "Worker's Song" and relates the struggle of a people whose sweat and strength helped "start the factory humming," and who "work late" to "keep the whole world running."

Poets sometimes separate themselves from the poem by assuming a personality or sex other than their own. Asked if she is the speaker in each poem, Angelou responded: "I hope I am the speaker. Sometimes it's my grandmother or a younger Maya, who I am now—and maybe who I hope not to be in the future."

The poem "Our Grandmothers" is one of the most poignant ones in the book. It is the focal point of a collection that testifies to the undaunted spirit of oppressed people everywhere. In it, the speaker relates the struggles of a mother trying to overcome her enslavement. As she lifts her head "a nod toward freedom" and exclaims "I shall not, I shall not be moved," the poem relates her story and that of her progeny.

"The use of the pronoun is significant. The poem refers to all grandmothers—Native American, Irish, European, African, Jewish, etc.—and their struggles to overcome obstacles. It's everybody's grandmother fighting for the right to be," the writer noted.

"I Shall Not Be Moved" relates a history of hard work, pain, joy, and the affection and heartbreak often associated with love.

"Coleridge Jackson," another significant poem in the collection, relates the plight of a man who "wouldn't take tea for the fever." Co-workers, friends and family tread softly around this man, yet his employer transforms him into a sniveling yes man. Rather than stand up to his "puny boss," Jackson takes out his frustration by beating family members. The writer's realistic description of the protagonist's plight, and his boss' gleeful reaction to the suffering he causes, offers the reader insight into the problems faced by numerous people who find it impossible to express their frustrations creatively.

Speaking about the impact of that particular poem, Angelou said: "I read that poem in public. And a young black man came up to me and thanked me. He said: 'Now I understand my father.' We hugged each other and cried."

In the poem titled "Love Letter," the speaker talks of the power of love. "Power," Angelou noted, "is a metaphor for strength but not the kind that gives you power over another human being. It addresses the strength to be yourself in a relationship and to be an equal in a love affair."

"Unfortunately," she added "that does not always last, but when you experience that kind of power, it can be an uplifting experience."

The poem "Human Family" best sums up what the poet is trying to relate throughout the work. The speaker says, "We are more alike, my friends, than we are different."

"I believe that we will have to get rid of the ogre of ignorance—bigotry—that keeps us from recognizing our similarities, or the human race will perish. And, if we don't, maybe it should!"

—Michele Howe, "Angelou's Poetry Builds Bridges Between Peoples." *Star–Ledger* (Newark, N. J.), June 3, 1990: p. C4.

Critical Views on
Maya Angelou's Poetry in General

LYNN Z. BLOOM ON DIFFERENT FEMALE PERSPECTIVES
IN ANGELOU'S LYRICS

[In this excerpt written for *Dictionary of Literary Biography
African-American Writers after 1955,* Lynn Bloom discusses
different female perspectives in Maya Angleou's lyrics.]

Angelou's three slim volumes of poetry, *Just Give Me a Cool Drink of
Water 'fore I Diiie* (1971, which incorporates many of the lyrics from
the 1969 recording of *The Poetry of Maya Angelou*), *Oh Pray My
Wings Are Gonna Fit Me Well* (1975), and *And Still I Rise* (1978), are
of lesser stature than her autobiographical writing.

Much of Angelou's poetry, almost entirely short lyrics, expresses
in strong, often jazzy rhythms, themes common to the life experiences of many American blacks—discrimination, exploitation,
being on welfare. Some of her poems extol the survivors, those
whose black pride enables them to prevail over the otherwise
demeaning circumstances of their existence. Thus in "When I Think
About Myself" she adopts the persona of an aging domestic to com-
ment ironically about the phenomenon of black survival in a world
dominated by whites: "Sixty years in these folks' world / The child I
works for calls me girl / I say 'Yes ma'am' for workings' sake. / Too
proud to bend / Too poor to break." In "Times-Square-Shoeshine-
Composition," the feisty black shoeshine boy defends, in dialect, his
thirty-five-cent price against the customer who tries to cheat him
out of a dime, his slangy remarks punctuated by the aggressive
"pow pow" of the shoeshine rag.

Other poems deal with social issues and problems which, though
not unique to blacks, are explored from a black perspective. In
"Letter to an Aspiring Junkie," a street-smart cat cautions the
prospective junkie to beware, "Climb into the streets, man, like you
climb / into the ass end of a lion." Angelou sympathizes with the
plight of abandoned black children, embodied in "John J," whose
"momma didn't want him," and who ends up gambling in a bar with
a "flinging singing lady." Her superficial look at "Prisoners" shows
them predictably experiencing "the horror / of gray guard men"—

"It's jail / and bail / then rails to run." At her most irritating, Angelou preaches. In language and hortatory tone reminiscent of popular turn-of-the-century poetry, she advises readers to "Take Time Out" to "show some kindness / for the folks / who thought that blindness / was an illness that / affected eyes alone."

When Angelou's lyrics deal with the common experiences of licit and illicit love, and of youth and aging, she writes from various female perspectives similar to those Dorothy Parker often used, and with Parker's self-consciousness, but without her wit. For example, in "Communication I" the lovelorn damsel, impervious to her wooer's quotations from Pope, Shaw, and Salinger, "frankly told her mother / 'Of all he said I understood, / he said he loved another.'" In mundane imagery ("The day hangs heavy / loose and grey / when you're away") a comparable persona laments her lover's evasiveness (Won't you pull yourself together / For / Me / ONCE"). And she screams at the silent "Telephone," "Ring. Damn you!" Her occasional vivid black dialect ("But forty years of age . . . / stomps / no-knocking / into the script / bumps a funky grind on the / shabby curtain of youth. . . .") enlivens expressions that seldom rise above the banal. Her poems seem particularly derivative and cloying when expressed in conventional language: "My pencil halts / and will not go / along that quiet path / I need to write / of lovers false. . . ."

Angelou's poetry becomes far more interesting when she dramatizes it in her characteristically dynamic stage performances. Angelou's statuesque figure, dressed in bright colors (and sometimes, African designs), moves exuberantly, vigorously to reinforce the rhythm of the lines, the tone of the words. Her singing and dancing and electrifying stage presence transcend the predictable words and rhymes.

—Lynn Z. Bloom, "Maya Angelou," in *Dictionary of Literary Biography*, vol. 38 (Detroit: Gale, 1985): pp. 10–11.

WILLIAM SYLVESTER ON THE "SASSINESS" OF ANGELOU'S POETRY

[In this passage William Sylvester writes about the astonishing rhythms of Maya Angelou's poems.]

In a BBC broadcast, Maya Angelou sang, unaccompanied, impromptu, two versions of the song "When the Saints Come Marching In"—this was after the publication of *Now Sheba Sings the Song*. First she sang with bright, cheerful surface, the "way whites do" and then she sang with a deep contralto "from the soul," drawing upon the music that flows deep within us all.

> . . . I rest somewhere
> between the unsung notes of night

as she phrased it in the title poem of *Shaker, Why Don't You Sing?* She evokes the unsung notes from her own experience "Awakening in New York," "A Georgia Sky," and reaches an "Unmeasured Tempo" for everybody with her wide, deep range of sympathies.

William Shakespeare was Angelou's "first white love," but her poems must be heard against a background of black rhythms. She has an uncanny ability to capture the sound of a voice on a page: *Just Give Me a Cool Drink of Water 'fore I Diiie:* vocal, oral, and written aspects blend in her poetry.

Ironically her own triumphs have drawn attention from the uniqueness of her poetry: she was named by Dr. Martin Luther King to be Northern Coordinator for his Southern Christian Fellowship, and by President Carter to be a member of the Commission for the International Women's Year. She has adapted Sophocles' *Ajax,* written for stage, TV, and films; she appeared in Genet's *The Blacks,* and had a highly successful career as a dancer. Her books have sold in the millions, but her poetry has received little serious critical attention.

In one sense of the word, however, her poetry is not "serious"; rather it is, as she herself puts it in the title poem of her volume *And Still I Rise,* "sassy." The word, however, has a powerful meaning: "sassy" implies—we should assume from her own words—that "the impudent child was detested by God, and a shame to its parents and could bring destruction to its house . . ." This use of litotes is congenial with a peculiar sot of "coding" as in the kenning. "God's candle bright" is more of a token for the "sun" than a metaphor. So too, the title of her autobiography, *I Know Why the Caged Bird Sings,* is not a sentimental metaphor, but a litotes for humiliation. In her poetry, understatement is a style for presenting a shared experience, in its inconsistency and its energy, and the "coding" can reinforce the anger implied by the "humor" as in "Sepia Fashion Show":

> Their hair, pomaded, faces jaded
> bones protruding, hip-wise,
> The models strutted, backed and butted,
> Then stuck their mouths out, lip-wise.
>
> They'd nasty manners, held like banners,
> while they looked down their nose-wise,
> I'd see 'em in hell, before they'd sell
> me one thing they're wearing, clothes-wise.
>
> The Black Bourgeois, who all say "yah"
> When yeah is what they're meaning
> Should look around, both up and down
> before they set out preening.
>
> "Indeed" they swear, "that's what I'll wear
> When I go country-clubbing,"
> I'd remind them please, look at those knees
> you got a Miss Ann's scrubbing.

The last line strikes the ear as "comic," and we share that sense of it, but then we react, and remember that black women literally had to show their knees to prove how hard they had cleaned. That change—the hearing, and then the reaction—is central to her poetry. We read the understated "nothing happens" in "Letter to an Aspiring Junkie," and then realize that it is a smashing litotes for "violence is everywhere":

> Let me hip you to the streets,
> Jim,
> Ain't nothing happening.
> Maybe some tomorrows gone up in smoke,
> raggedy preachers, telling a joke
> to lonely, son-less old ladies' maids.
>
> Nothing happening,
> Nothing shakin', Jim.
> A slough of young cats riding that
> cold, white horse,

a grey old monkey on their back, of course
does rodeo tricks.

No haps, man.
No haps.
A worn-out pimp, with a space-age conk,
setting up some fool for a game of tonk,
or poker or
get 'em dead and alive.

The streets?
Climb into the streets man, like you climb
into the ass end of a lion.
Then it's fine.
It's a bug-a-loo and a shing-a-ling,
African dreams on a buck-and-a-wing and a prayer.
That's the streets man,
Nothing happening.

The experience is particular: the word "conk" means a hair-do (rather like Little Richard's, for example) but the energy comes from the astonishing rhythms, and perhaps more accurately from the changes of rhythm.

Angelou has composed poetry from the particulars and the rhythms she knows, and the changes of rhythm become a rhythm, the upsets and restarts in an unsteady state of soul which every life has experienced in some place or other.

When we read Angelou's poetry we share the sense of it, but then we have a reaction from the energy, and have to reassess it, so that ultimately, when we hear her poetry, we listen to ourselves.

—William Sylvester, "Maya Angelou," in *Contemporary Poets* (Chicago: St. James Press, 1985): pp. 19–20.

GEORGE PLIMPTON: INTERVIEW WITH MAYA ANGELOU

[In this excerpt from George Plimpton's interview with Maya Angelou, published in *Paris Review* in 1990, the author discusses the way that she writes.]

INTERVIEWER

⟨H⟩ow do you start a day's work?

ANGELOU

I have kept a hotel room in every town I've ever lived in. I rent a hotel room for a few months, leave my home at six and try to be at work by 6:30. To write, I lie across the bed, so that this elbow is absolutely encrusted at the end, just so rough with callouses. I never allow the hotel people to change the bed, because I never sleep there. I stay until 12:30 or 1:30 in the afternoon, and then I go home and try to breathe; I look at the work around five; I have an orderly dinner: proper, quiet, lovely dinner; and then I go back to work the next morning. Sometimes in hotels I'll go into the room, and there'll be a note on the floor which says, "Dear Miss Angelou, let us change the sheets. We think they are moldy." But I only allow them to come in and empty wastebaskets. I insist that all things are taken off the walls. I don't want anything in there. I go into the room, and I feel as if all my beliefs are suspended. Nothing holds me to anything. No milkmaids, no flowers, nothing. I just want to *feel* and then when I start to work I'll remember. I'll read something, maybe the Psalms, maybe, again, something from Mr. Dunbar, James Weldon Johnson. And I'll remember how beautiful, how pliable the language is, how it will lend itself. If you pull it, it says, "Okay." I remember that, and I start to write. Nathaniel Hawthorne says, "Easy reading is damn hard writing." I try to pull the language in to such a sharpness that it jumps off the page. It must look easy, but it takes me forever to get it to look so easy. Of course, there are those critics—New York critics as a rule—who say, "Well, Maya Angelou has a new book out and, of course, it's good but then she's a natural writer." Those are the ones I want to grab by the throat and wrestle to the floor because it takes me forever to get it to sing. I *work* at the language. On an evening like this, looking out at the auditorium, if I had to write this evening from my point of view, I'd see the rust-red used worn velvet seats, and the lightness where people's backs have rubbed against the back of the seat so that it's a light orange; then, the beautiful colors of the people's faces, the white, pink-white, beige-white, light beige and brown and tan—I would have to look at all that, at all those faces and the way they sit on top of their necks. When I would end up writing after four hours or five hours in my room, it might sound like: "It was a rat that sat on a mat. That's that. Not a cat." But I would continue to play with it and pull at it and say, "I love you. Come to me. I love you." It might take me two or three weeks just to describe what I'm seeing now.

INTERVIEWER

How do you know when it's what you want?

ANGELOU

I know when it's the best I can do. It may not be the best there is. Another writer may do it much better. But I know when it's the best I can do. I know that one of the great arts that the writer develops is the art of saying, "No. No, I'm finished. Bye." And leaving it alone. I will not write it into the ground. I will not write the life out of it. I won't do that.

INTERVIEWER

How much revising is involved?

ANGELOU

I write in the morning, and then go home about midday and take a shower, because writing, as you know, is very hard work, so you have to do a double ablution. Then I go out and shop—I'm a serious cook—and pretend to be normal. I play sane: "Good morning! Fine, thank you. And you?" And I go home. I prepare dinner for myself and if I have houseguests, I do the candles and the pretty music and all that. Then, after all the dishes are moved away, I read what I wrote that morning. And more often than not, if I've done nine pages I may be able to save two and a half, or three. That's the cruelest time you know, to really admit that it doesn't work. And to blue pencil it. When I finish maybe fifty pages, and read them—fifty acceptable pages—it's not too bad. I've had the same editor since 1967. Many times he has said to me over the years, or asked me, "Why would you use a semi-colon instead of a colon?" And many times over the years I have said to him things like: "I will never speak to you again. Forever. Goodbye. That is it. Thank you very much." And I leave. Then I read the piece and I think of his suggestions. I send him a telegram that says, "OK, so you're right. So what? Don't ever mention this to me again. If you do, I will never speak to you again." About two years ago I was visiting him and his wife in the Hamptons. I was at the end of a dining room table with a sit-down dinner of about fourteen people. Way at the end I said to someone, "I sent him telegrams over the years." From the other end of the table he said, "And I've kept every one!" Brute! But the editing, one's own editing, before the editor sees it, is the most important.

—George Plimpton, "The Art of Fiction CXIX: Maya Angelou," *Paris Review* 32, no. 116 (1990): pp. 149–51.

LYMAN B. HAGEN ON THE "LIGHT" VERSE OF ANGELOU'S POETRY

[Lyman B. Hagen devotes several pages to Maya Angelou's poetry, discussing her themes, style, and diction.]

Angelou's poems are a continuum of mood and emotion. They go from the excitement of love to outrage over racial injustice, from the pride of blackness and African heritage to suffered slurs. Angelou follows Countee Cullen's literary perspective that black authors have the prerogative to "do, write, create what we will, our only concern being that we do it well and with all the power in us." Angelou indeed speaks out in many ways and with the best of words she can summon.

Angelou's poetry is generally brief, in the tradition of Langston Hughes who believed that a poem should be short—the shorter the better. Forty percent of the 135 poems in the Bantam edition are 15 lines or less. Of this forty percent, fifteen poems contain three stanzas, twelve have two stanzas, and eleven poems are unstructured. These eleven seem rather forced and rhetorical. Another dozen poems contain between eleven and fifteen lines each. The remainder of her 135 collected poems range from 30 to 50 lines. Angelou never indulges in lengthy narrative poems. She chooses words frugally. The length of line in her poems is also short. Most lines of her three-stanza poems are trimeter; others, particularly those in the unstructured poems, are from two to four syllables long. Some critics do cite her poetry as "oversimplistic or slight because of the short lines, easy diction, and heavy dependence on rhythm and rhyme in her poetry." But Angelou herself has frequently commented on the difficulty of reducing complex thoughts and ideas to a poetic format. She says she begins with many pages of words on her yellow legal pad and works long and hard at distilling them.

Total poetic meaning stresses both emotional content and rhythmical elements. If the emotional content can be considered the bricks of the poem, the rhythm would be the mortar that binds. Angelou is a natural builder of poetry for she not only has a keen sensitivity to feeling, but also a marvelous sense of rhythm. Her musical awareness is so strong that she claims she *hears* music in ordinary, everyday circumstances. A rhythmical awareness has been reinforced by four important influences on her: first, her many readings of the lyrical King James Bible; second, acknowledged reading of traditional white writers such as Edgar Allen Poe, William Thackeray, and particularly William Shakespeare; and of prominent black writers such as Paul Laurence Dunbar, Langston Hughes, James Weldon Johnson, Countee Cullen, and of W.E.B. Du Bois' "Litany at Atlanta." A third strong influence grew out of her participation in the rhythmical shouting and singing in African-American church services with their emotional spirituals; and the strong, moving sermons preached in those churches, whose tones she absorbed into her being. The fourth shaping force derives from childhood chants, songs and rhyme games long familiar in folklore.

—Lyman B. Hagen, *Heart of a Woman, Mind of a Writer, and Soul of a Poet* (Lanham, Md.: University Press of America, 1997): pp. 118–120.

MARY JANE LUPTON ON THE POETS WHO INFLUENCED MAYA ANGELOU

[This chapter is taken from Mary Jane Lupton's book *Maya Angelou: A Critical Companion*. Here, Lupton writes about the poets who influenced Maya Angelou.]

While James Weldon Johnson and Frederick Douglass may have shaped her views about black narrative structures, it should also be emphasized that many of her literary heroes were poets, white and black, male and female. They influenced the way she wrote, thought, and imagined.

As a child, Angelou was affected by the ideas and rhythms of lyric poetry. In *Caged Bird* she is quite specific in acknowledging her debt to William Shakespeare, Edgar Allan Poe, and James Weldon Johnson. In the "Icon" interview of June 16, 1997, Angelou insisted that black women poets also affected her, although she does not acknowledge their influence in *Caged Bird*. She mentioned Georgia Douglas Johnson, a poet who wrote with emotion about gender and from whom she took the title of her fourth autobiography, *The Heart of a Woman*. Other black women poets Angelou admired when she was young were Frances Harper and Anne Spencer: "Frances Harper meant a lot to me. Georgia Douglas Johnson. Anne Spencer. And Jessie Fauset." Of these women writers, three were known as poets although Harper (1825–1911) is also remembered for her novels, especially for *Iola Leroy* (1895), the story of a woman of mixed race. Angelou quotes from Frances Harper's poem, "The Slave Auction," in one of the reflections that appears in *Even the Stars Look Lonesome*. Georgia Douglas Johnson wrote "The Heart of a Woman," the 1918 lyric that became the title of Angelou's fourth autobiography. Anne Spencer (1882–1975) appealed to Angelou for her poignant ballad, "Lady, Lady," about a servant whose hands had been bleached white from detergent, and for other ballads illustrating the oppression of black women. Finally, novelist Jessie Fauset (1884–1961) was literary editor of *The Crisis*, founded by W.E.B. Du Bois, a renowned black intellectual. Fauset was the most prolific novelist of the Harlem Renaissance (1919–1929), and one of its most educated spokespersons. It is possible that from Fauset Angelou obtained models for plot construction and character development, especially Fauset's reliance on the mother / child motif.

When she was young, Angelou was intrigued by several white women poets. She appreciated the romantic and lyrical qualities of Emily Dickinson (1830–1886), and echoes of Dickinson's familiar ballad form can be heard in some of Angelou's poems. She also enjoyed the passion of Edna St. Vincent Millay (1892–1950) and the caustic humor of Dorothy Parker(1893–1967): "They are funny and wry," she remarked in appreciation of Millay and Parker. "I'm rarely wry. I think I'm funny. I love to be funny."

When asked about the influence of African and Asian poets on her work she clearly acknowledged Kwesi Brew, the Ghanaian poet who appears in *All God's Children Need Traveling Shoes:* "Oh yes," she said, "Kwesi influenced me and still does. But the early influences, I had no idea African poets even existed early on." She explained that African poets were not published in the United States while she was growing up. One of the first African poets who came to her attention was Senegalese statesman Leopold Senghor, and that was not until she was an adult. She was more familiar with Chinese and Japanese poets than with African poets because they were available. Some of her poetry has been influenced by the Japanese haiku, a poetic description written in three lines totalling seventeen syllables.

Angelou's autobiographies are informed not only by her experiments in poetic form but also by her journey into Asian, African, and African American literature. In her view, anyone who emerges from the journey of life is an autobiographer. She thus draws all of God's children into her encompassing definition of what makes an autobiographer: "Each one is an autobiographer. . . . So I think we're all on journeys, according to how we're able to travel, overcome, undercome, and share what we have learned."

—Mary Jane Lupton, *Maya Angelou: A Critical Companion* (Westport, Conn.: Greenwood Press, 1998): pp. 48–50.

Thematic Analysis of
"When I Think About Myself"

The poem is published in the volume of poetry *Just Give Me a Cool Drink of Water 'Fore I Diiie,* which included many of the lyrics from Maya Angelou's 1969 recording of the *Poetry of Maya Angelou.* When published in 1971, the book was nominated for the Pulitzer Prize. There are 38 poems in the book, among them some of her best known, such as: "Harlem Hopscotch," "Miss Scarlett, Mr. Rhett and Other Latter Day Saints," and "The Gamut." The volume consists of two parts: The first, "Where Love Is a Scream of Anguish," includes 20 poems that deal with love and its joys and losses. In the second part, entitled "Just Before the World Ends," Maya Angelou turns her attention to the lives of black people in America from the time of slavery to the rebellious 1960s. According to the reviewer, Chad Walsh, "the second part has more bite, the anguished and often sardonic expression of a black in a white-dominated world."

The influence of African American poets through the oral tradition of spirituals like "Roll, Jordan Roll" and the written poetry of James Weldon Johnson, Langston Hughes, and Jean Toomer can be traced in this poem.

The first stanza of this protest poem opens with "When I think about myself, I almost laugh to death"; the "I" is not identified. Only indefinite judgments on life are revealed: the speaker's life has been one great joke, "a dance that is walked" (instead of danced) and a "song that's spoke" (instead of sung). The stanza ends with lines that will, slightly modified, close each of three stanzas of this poem:

> I laugh so hard I almost choke
> When I think about myself.

The second stanza tells us more about the persona of the poem. She is 60 years old, poor, a black woman who works probably as a maid for a younger white woman. The white woman, in an astutely degrading way, addresses her as "girl":

> Sixty years in these folks' world
> The child I works for call me girl
>   I say "Yes ma'am" for working sake.

In a poignant line she announces that she is "too proud to bend" and "too poor to break." This time she laughs until her stomach aches, when she thinks about herself.

In the third stanza the movement shifts to her folks—in other words, African Americans. At the thought of their helpless status the persona of the poem almost dies of laughing. Two lines firmly explicate the social injustice carried out on her people:

> They grow the fruit
> But are allowed to eat only the rind.

The speaker's personal lament expands into a song of general protest. The poem closes with the lines "I laugh until I start crying / When I think about my folks." The defense mechanism of laughter cannot hold the real emotions anymore.

Some African traditions hold that if the soul (*sunsum*) is hurt or wounded it will, before long, make the body sick. Music and laughter are used as a psychological release to prevent illness as a result of sick sunsum. Maya Angelou in an interview said that the woman in this poem "laughs to shield her crying." We can try to replace "laugh" throughout the poem with "cry," and we will capture the more authentic meaning of the poem. Nonetheless, the woman cries without surrendering to self-pity, thus permitting the poem to become the voice of her people, striking at the heart of their consciousness. ❀

Critical Views on
"When I Think About Myself"

PRISCILLA R. RAMSEY ON THE "I" OF AFRICAN-AMERICAN
POETRY

[Priscilla R. Ramsey is a professor at the Department of
Afro-American Studies at Howard University (Washington,
D.C.). In this extract on the poem "When I Think About
Myself," she focuses on the "I" of African-American poetry,
and "I" that is not a singular pronoun but a collective
symbol for an entire people.]

A self-defining function continues in "When I Think About Myself."
We hear the definitions through a narrative she frequently uses in
her poetry: Angelou's persona assumes an ironic distance toward the
world. As a result, her relationship to the world loses its direct, i.e.,
literal quality. She steps back into this distance and can laugh at its
characteristics no matter how politically and socially devastating:

When I Think About Myself

When I think about myself
I almost laugh myself to death.
My life has been one big joke.
A dance that's walked
A song that's spoke,
I laugh so hard I almost choke
When I think about myself.

Sixty years in these folks' world
The child I works for calls me girl.
I say "Yes Ma'am" for working's sake
Too proud to bend,
Too poor to break.
I laugh until my stomach ache,
When I think about myself.

My folks can make me split my sides,
I laughed so hard I nearly died,
The tales they tell, sound just like lying,
They grow the fruit,
But eat the rind,
I laugh until I start to crying,
When I think about my folks.

Out of the emotional distance comes the paradox upon which the persona's insights rest. Dances are walked and songs are spoken reinforcing the dialectical nature of this paradox: an illusion which keeps sacrosanct a much more complicated racial reality.

Both Stephen Henderson's *Understanding the New Black Poetry* and Ruth Sheffey argue that the "I" of Black poetry is not a singular or individualistic referent but a symbol for the ideas of a Black collective. With that point in mind, it becomes clear she is ultimately talking about the ironies of economic oppression which trap Black people provided they allow them, i.e., the ironies to define them rather than their gaining the distance from the oppression to define themselves. An unending tension exists between haves and have-nots—one which the have-nots cannot allow to erupt into open violence and conflict (excluding certain mass exceptions like Watts, New York and Washington in the 1960's). Having once gained an understanding of the absurdity, the have-nots gain superiority in that ironic distance which creates freedom and a partial definition of one's superiority over the oppressor's blind myopia. Perhaps as a further illumination of the ideas generating this poem, Maya Angelou told an illustrative story to George Goodman, Jr. who was reviewing her autobiography, "Caged Bird" for the *New York Times*. He remarked that Angelou consistently expressed the sickness of racism like a thread running throughout all her work. Her reply took an illustrative form as she told him about an elderly Black domestic worker in Montgomery, Alabama during Martin Luther King's 1955 Montgomery bus boycotts. The worker solemnly assured her white employer that in spite of the boycotts, she had instructed her husband and children to ride the daily busses. Afterwards, behind the closed, protective doors of the kitchen the employer's liberal, more realistic daughter asked the Black woman why she needed to hide the truth (the Black woman had, in reality, told her family to absolutely stay away from public transportation busses in Montgomery). The elderly maid (a prototype not divorced from this poem's persona by any flight of the imagination) told her, "Honey when you have your head in a lion's mouth, you don't jerk it out. You scratch him behind the ears and draw it out gradually." Like the conclusion of the woman's story, this persona speaks a similarly paradigmatic truth in all its ironic and varied implications. Psychological distance becomes the persona's mightiest weapon, a distance born of years of slowly drawing one's head out of the proverbial lion's mouth.

—Priscilla R. Ramsey, "Transcendence: The Poetry of Maya Angelou," *A Current Bibliography on African Affairs* 17 (1984–85): pp. 144–46.

KATHY M. ESSICK ON ONE'S SELF-PRIDE

[This extract is taken from Kathy M. Essick's dissertation on poetry by Maya Angelou, published by Indiana University of Pennsylvania in 1994. Here she asserts that the theme of one's self-exultation and self-pride is prevailing in this poem.]

In "When I Think About Myself," the speaker cries out against a system that supports the economic oppression of blacks by whites. The persona is a sixty-year-old poor black woman who works as a maid for a very young white woman who addresses her as "girl." As a defense mechanism to dismiss her suffering, she ironically laughs at herself and the life of lack that she endures. She likens her life to "a dance that's walked [and] a song that's spoke." She laughs also at the injustices suffered by her family members who have been denied the fruits of their arduous labors which produce abundant crops for the white landowner while her family barely survives on the scraps. But this "laughter" chokes the speaker and causes her stomach to sink. Then the laughter gives over to crying. Even though the speaker unquestionably suffers pain from the social injustices, she perserveres, "Too proud to bend / Too poor to break." Priscilla Ramsey says the speaker laughs at the political and social injustices in order to achieve emotional distance. She also sees this poem as "a self-defining function" for the poet. Even though the speaker of the poem cries at the end, she does not surrender to self-pity. Many of Angelou's protest poems (and almost all of the poems in Part Two of *Cool Drink*) center on the theme of one's self-exultation and self-pride that prevent one from losing her will in spite of experiences involving pain and degradation.

—Kathy M. Essick, *The Poe*
Matrix as Force and Code (.
Pennsylvania, 1994): pp. 125–2

LYMAN B. HAGEN ON THE SERVI WOMAN

[Lyman B. Hagen is the author of
Woman, Mind of a Writer, and Soul
Analysis of the Writings of Maya Angelo
Hagen discusses Angelou's sentimen
woman from the poem.]

Angelou comes to the defense of Uncle Tom:
black activists because they do not overtly resist
"When I Think About Myself," Angelou explains
responds with a simple "Yes, ma'am" for the sake
young white who insults her with the offensive w
vant does not pity herself and knows she is keeping
being servile for an entire lifetime, she has provide
another generation who may find better conditi
appropriate, Angelou voices approval of those who en
ties to feed, shelter, clothe, and educate the family.

—Lyman B. Hagen, *Heart of a Woman, Mind of a Write*
Poet (Lanham, Md.: University Press of America, 1997):

Thematic Analysis of
...mes-Square-Shoeshine-Composition"

...em appeared in the volume of poetry entitled *Just Give Me a ...rink of Water 'Fore I Diiie,* Part Two, in 1971.

... shoeshine boy's proud boasting of his talents opens the poem:

...m the best that ever done it
...pow, pow)
    that's my title and I won it
    (pow, pow)
I ain't lying, I'm the best
(pow, pow)
    Come and put me to the test.
    (pow, pow)

...e onomatopoeic repetitive "pow, pow" comes after each line.

The boy captures the reader with his openness. He cleans the ...oes till they squeak, and he promises he will shine them till they ...hine. In the third stanza, he is not up to bargaining about his price with the owner of the shoes. If he insists on bartering his charge of "a quarter and a dime" to "a quarter," he can give it to his daughter.

The first line of the fourth stanza—"I ain't playing dozens mister"—alludes to the game in which participants insult each other or each other's relatives, looks, or life situation. The objective of the game is to endure the offenses as long as possible without losing one's temper. The first person who gives in to anger is the loser; the winner is the person who is able to keep her composure.

The shoeshine boy humorously and mockingly closes the poem by saying:

Say I'm like a greedy bigot
(pow, pow)
    I'm a cap'tilist, can you dig it?
    (pow, pow)

The poem echoes the blues/protest poetry of Langston Hughes. In fact, a close reading and analysis of Angelou's poems suggest that a blues-based model may provide an instrument for examining the variety of subjects, style, themes, and use of vernacular in Angelou's poems.

The name "blues" has been bestowed on a style of songs with themes and feelings of being "blue" or sad. African-American blues music ordinarily reflects unhappiness that ranges from minor irritations to great suffering. The blues singer achieves control of his emotions that seem to be self-defeating by using laughter or ridicule instead of tears to cope with his immediate contingencies.

Angelou uses this same technique in this poem, as she does in much of her other poetry. ❁

Critical Views on
"Times-Square-Shoeshine-Composition"

CAROL E. NEUBAUER ON "TIMES-SQUARE-SHOESHINE-COMPOSITION" AND "HARLEM HOPSCOTCH"

[In this extract, taken from her essay on Maya Angelou, Carol E. Neubauer compares two poems that, according to her, embody Angelou's belief that the situation must improve for African Americans.]

Two poems that embody the poet's confident determination that conditions must improve for the black race are "Times-Square-Shoeshine-Composition" and "Harlem Hopscotch." Both ring with a lively, invincible beat that carries defeated figures into at least momentary triumph. "Times-Square" tells the story of a shoeshine man who claims to be an unequaled master at his trade. He cleans and shines shoes to a vibrant rhythm that sustains his spirit in spite of humiliating circumstances. When a would-be customer offers him twenty-five cents instead of the requested thirty-five cents, the shoeshine man refuses the job and flatly renounces the insulting attempt to minimize the value of his trade. Fully appreciating his own expertise, the vendor proudly instructs his potential Times Square patron to give his measly quarter to his daughter, sister, or mamma, for they clearly need it more than he does. Denying the charge that he is a "greedy bigot," the shoeshine man simply admits that he is a striving "capitalist," trying to be successful in a city owned by the superrich.

Moving uptown, "Harlem Hopscotch" celebrates the sheer strength necessary for survival. The rhythm of this powerful poem echoes the beat of feet, first hopping, then suspended in air, and finally landing in the appropriate square. To live in a world measured by such blunt announcements as "food is gone" and "the rent is due," people need to be extremely energetic and resilient. Compounding the pressures of hunger, poverty, and unemployment is the racial bigotry that consistently discriminates against people of color. Life itself has become a brutal game of hopscotch, a series of desperate yet hopeful leaps, landing but never pausing long: "In the air, now both feet down. / Since you black, don't stick around." Yet in the final analysis, the words that bring the poem and the complete collection to a close triumphantly announce the poet's victory: "Both feet flat, the game is done. / They think I lost. I think I won." These poems in their sensitive treatment of both love and black identity are the poet's own defense against the incredible odds in the game of life.

> —Carol E. Neubauer, "Maya Angelou: Self and a Song of Freedom in the Southern Tradition," *Southern Women Writers: The New Generation,* ed. Tonette Bond Inge (Tuscaloosa: University of Alabama Press, 1990): pp. 133–34.

KATHY M. ESSICK ON THE VERNACULAR LANGUAGE IN THE POEM

[This extract is taken from Kathy M. Essick's dissertation on Maya Angelou's poetry, published by Indiana University of Pennsylvania in 1994. Here Essick demonstrates the poet's control of the vernacular language.]

In "Times-Square-Shoeshine-Composition" (*Just Give Me a Cool Drink of Water 'fore I Diiie,* Part Two), the speaker, a shoeshine boy, like the earlier singing workers, relies on the rhythm and repetition of his song to maintain his pace as well as to relieve the boredom of his labors, while the language and rhythm in the song imitate the sound of his work. This is especially true of the repetitive onomatopoeia, "pow pow," punctuating each line of the poem. This poetic effect imitates the sound of the movement of the shoeshine boy's cloth across his patron's shoes. Likewise, the sound of the alternating lines, here used for communicating information, imitates the rhythm of the cloth at work, while the lyrics provide the shoeshine boy a vehicle to boast of his talents and abilities:

I'm the best that ever done it
(pow pow)
     that's my title and I won it
     (pow pow)
I ain't lying, I'm the best
(pow pow)
     Come and put me to the test
     (pow pow).

Throughout the poem, the speaker demonstrates his control of the vernacular language. His use of repetition and difference to convey meaning is an example of what Henry Louis Gates, Jr. identifies as the guiding principle in African-American discourse—Signifyin(g). Through the clever, rhetorical language of the trickster figure, the shoeshine boy "Signifies" upon his tale in front of potential customers in a verbal play of figurative elements.

The speaker also "Signifies" on the "dozens," perhaps the most well-known subsets of Signifyin(g) in which the participants engage in a verbal fusilade of insults directed at each others' relatives, appearance or situation. The object of the "dozens" game is to maintain emotional control; the first person to give into anger is the loser. The speaker in this poem advertises that he will "clean 'em til they squeak" and "shine 'em til they whine"; therefore, he says that he is not open to bartering his price through the verbal dueling game, "the dozens." Because of the indeterminant nature of Signifyin(g) which achieves its effect through indirect and ambiguous argumentation, it could be suggested that the shoeshine boy in this case actually welcomes "dozens" playing:

> For a quarter and a dime
> (pow pow)
>> You can get the dee luxe shine
>> (pow pow)
> Say you wanta pay a quarter?
> (pow pow)
>> Then you give that to your daughter
>> (pow pow)
> I ain't playing dozens mister
> (pow pow).

In the final stanza the shoeshine boy audaciously defends his stance and identifies himself as "cap'tilist":

> Say I'm like a greedy bigot
> (pow pow)
>> I'm a cap'tilist, can you dig it?
>> (pow pow).

Again, the shoeshine boy speaks as a trickster figure, here using catchy rhyme and rhythm to achieve humor in Signifyin(g) meaning upon greed, bigotry and capitalism. In this way Angelou satirizes the capitalistic system that enslaved and oppressed her people. Her use of irony at the end—that the shoeshine boy would espouse the capitalistic system—is characteristic of many poems in Part Two of *Just Give Me a Cool Drink of Water 'fore I Diiie.*

—Kathy M. Essick, *The Poetry of Maya Angelou: A Study of the Blues Matrix as Force and Code* (Indiana, Penn.: Indiana University of Pennsylvania, 1994): pp. 66–69.

Thematic Analysis of
"Phenomenal Woman"

This poem is considered one of the best poems in the collection *And Still I Rise* (1978), which is Maya Angelou's third book of poetry. The volume consists of 32 poems divided into three chapters: "Touch Me, Life, Not Softly," "Trembling" and "And Still I Rise."

"Phenomenal Woman" was featured also in John Singleton's 1993 movie *Poetic Justice,* in a story about a young black woman (played by Janet Jackson), who deals with issues of loss and survival. (Angelou also has a brief role as a family member at a reunion.)

In this hymn-like poem to woman's beauty, the self-confident speaker reveals her attributes as a phenomenal woman. Unlike the fashion magazines' beauties, she exults in being different:

> Pretty women wonder where my secret lies.
> I'm not cute or built to suit a fashion model's size

Then she catalogues her strengths:

> It's in the reach of my arms,
> The span of my hips,
> The stride of my step,
> The curl of my lips.

> Each of four stanzas closes with the robust refrain:

> I'm a woman
> Phenomenally.
> Phenomenal woman.
> That's me.

Angelou skillfully plays with the word "phenomenal": it can denote something of the nature of phenomena, something perceived by the senses or through immediate experience. The word "phenomenally," on the other hand, means remarkably, extraordinarily, exceedingly.

In the moving second stanza, the speaker continues to enumerate the charms of her femininity, which overwhelm men. This time she ascribes her appeal to the fire in her eyes and flash of her teeth, the swing of her waist and the joy of her feet.

There is a shift of stress in the third stanza. Now, not only her physical beauty but her inner mystery attracts men.

> Men themselves have wondered
> What they see in me.
> They try so much
> But they can't touch
> My inner mystery.

This mystery lies in the arch of her back, in the sun of her smile, in the rise of her breasts, and the grace of her style.

This self-image, full of glory, inner pride, and innate individuality, asserts itself in the last stanza:

> When you see me passing
> It ought to make you proud.
> I say,
> It's in the click of my heels,
> The bend of my hair,
> The palm of my hand,
> The need for my care.

The poem is enormously popular among common readers despite scarce reviews by critics. The lines are said to release astonishing vigor in Angelou's characteristically dynamic stage performances. ❀

Critical Views on
"Phenomenal Woman"

CAROL E. NEUBAUER ON WOMAN'S VITALITY IN "PHE-
NOMENAL WOMAN" AND "WOMAN WORK"

[In this extract, taken from her essay on Maya Angelou,
Carol E. Neubauer asserts that "Phenomenal Woman"
praises woman's vitality.]

As the title of Maya Angelou's third volume of poetry, *And Still I
Rise,* suggests, this collection contains a hopeful determination to
rise above discouraging defeat. These poems are inspired and spoken
by a confident voice of strength that recognizes its own power and
will no longer be pushed into passivity. The book consists of thirty-
two poems, which are divided into three sections, "Touch Me, Life,
Not Softly," "Traveling," and "And Still I Rise." Two poems, "Phenomenal Woman" and "Just for a Time" appeared in *Cosmopolitan* in
1978. Taken as a whole, this series of poems covers a broader range
of subjects than the earlier two volumes and shifts smoothly from
issues such as springtime and aging to sexual awakening, drug addiction, and Christian salvation. The familiar themes of love and its
inevitable loneliness and the oppressive climate of the South are still
central concerns. But even more striking than the poet's careful
treatment of these subjects is her attention to the nature of woman
and the importance of family.

One of the best poems in this collection is "Phenomenal Woman,"
which captures the essence of womanhood and at the same time
describes the many talents of the poet herself. As is characteristic of
Angelou's poetic style, the lines are terse and forcefully, albeit irregu-
larly, rhymed. The words themselves are short, often monosyllabic,
and collectively create an even, provocative rhythm that resounds
with underlying confidence. In four different stanzas, a woman
explains her special graces that make her stand out in a crowd and
attract the attention of both men and women, although she is not,
by her own admission, "cut or built to suit a fashion model's size."
One by one, she enumerates her gifts, from "the span of my hips" to
"the curl of my lips," from "the flash of my teeth" to "the joy in my
feet." Yet her attraction is not purely physical; men seek her for her
"inner mystery," "the grace of [her] style," and "the need for [her]

care." Together each alluring part adds up to a phenomenal woman who need not "bow" her head but can walk tall with a quiet pride that beckons those in her presence.

Similar to "Phenomenal Woman" in its economical form, strong rhyme scheme, and forceful rhythm is "Woman Work." The two poems also bear a thematic resemblance in their praise of woman's vitality. Although "Woman Work" does not concern the physical appeal of woman, as "Phenomenal Woman" does, it delivers a corresponding litany of the endless cycle of chores in a woman's typical day. In the first stanza, the long list unravels itself in forcefully rhymed couplets:

> I've got the children to tend
> The clothes to mend
> The floor to mop
> The food to shop
> Then the chicken to fry
> Then baby to dry.

Following the complete category of tasks, the poet adds four shorter stanzas, which reveal the source of woman's strength. This woman claims the sunshine, rain, and dew as well as storms, wind, and snow as her own. The dew cools her brow, the wind lifts her "across the sky," the snow covers her "with white / Cold icy kisses," all bringing her rest and eventually the strength to continue. For her, there is no other source of solace and consolation than nature and its powerful elements.

— Carol E. Neubauer, "Maya Angelou: Self and a Song of Freedom in the Southern Tradition," *Southern Women Writers: The New Generation*, ed. Tonette Bond Inge (Tuscaloosa: University of Alabama Press, 1990): pp. 136–37.

LYMAN B. HAGEN DEFENDS MAYA ANGELOU AGAINST THE CRITICS

[Lyman B. Hagen is the author of the book *Heart of a Woman, Mind of a Writer, and Soul of a Poet: A Critical Analysis of the Writings of Maya Angelou.* In this selection, Hagen acknowledges that Angelou has not always been taken seriously by the critics, but he defends her work against this criticism.]

Robert Loomis, Angelou's long-time editor at Random House, supports her with his well-taken remarks:

> I've always believed that those who have reservations about Angelou's poetry simply don't understand what she's doing. She is very strongly in a certain tradition of Black American poetry, and when I hear her read or declaim the works of other Black American poets, I can see very clearly what her heritage is and what her inspiration is. Furthermore, Maya is not writing the sort of poetry that most of us grew up in school admiring. What she is writing is poetry that is very definitely in what I would call the oral tradition. That is, what she writes can be read aloud and even acted. When her words are spoken, they are extremely effective and moving. They always sound just right.

Although few critics have found great merit in her poetry, Angelou has acquired a dedicated audience. Her work seems to have a special appeal to college students. At her public readings, a generally balanced cross-section, male and female, black and white, is in attendance. She delights and enchants the entire group with her timing and powerful delivery. Some admirers of her poetry have been so impressed with its rhymes, rhythms, and content that they themselves have been encouraged to write. Many poets manqué have sent Angelou their unsolicited creations. Quite a few of these can be found stored with her collected papers at the Wake Forest University library. Angelou encourages young people to express themselves openly and seeks to inspire them.

⟨. . .⟩ Angelou covers a wide range of subject matter. In Angelou's writings, poetry or prose, she holds to tradition and makes a special effort to dispel false impressions about African Americans, but does not use this as her sole motivation.

Angelou's poetry belongs in the category "light" verse. Her poems are entertainments derived from personal experiences and fall into one of two broad subject areas. First, she writes about everyday considerations—the telephone, aging, insomnia—topics that are totally neutral. Second, she writes with deep feeling about a variety of racial themes and concerns.

⟨. . .⟩ Sometimes Angelou uses contrasting pairs in her poetry. For example, in "Phenomenal Woman," considered a personal theme-poem, she asserts the special qualities of a particular woman. The woman described is easily matched to the author herself. Angelou is an imposing woman—at least six feet tall. She has a strong personality and a compelling presence as defined in the poem. One can accept the autobiographical details in this poem or extend the reading to infer that all women have qualities that attract attention. Angelou's dramatic presentation of this poem always pleases her audience and is frequently the highlight of her programs.

Angelou pairs this poem with "Men." The speaker is a woman whose experience has taught her the games men play. In this she uses a raw egg metaphor to contrast fragile femininity with dominant masculinity, but the female speaker has perhaps learned to be cautious.

⟨. . .⟩ Angelou's poems are dramatic and lyrical. Her style is open, direct, unambiguous, and conversational. The diction is plain but sometimes the metaphors are quite striking. The most successful of her poems are those that "have language close to speech or more nearly song," those written in the vernacular. ⟨. . .⟩

A knowledge of black linguistic regionalisms and folklore enhances the appreciation of Angelou's poems. Thus a Whorfian "linguistic relativity" in which language shapes the way we view the world may be at work here. But most of Angelou's poems can be understood and appreciated on their own merits, sans special insight. Her topics of simple universal concerns embrace the breadth of everyday worldly encounters, and, through poetic presentation, uplift these ordinary experiences to special status for the ordinary reader.

—Lyman B. Hagen, *Heart of a Woman, Mind of a Writer, and Soul of a Poet* (Lanham, Md.: University Press of America, 1997): pp. 123–24, 126, 130, 132.

Thematic Analysis of
"Still I Rise"

The title poem of the collection *And Still I Rise* (1978) describes the narrator's hopeful determination to rise above life's discouraging defeats.

Stephen Henderson's remark from *Understanding the New Black Poetry* is relevant to the reading of this poem; he explains that the "I" of African-American poetry is a not a singular or an individualistic referent but a symbol for the ideas of a black collective. With that in mind, we can better understand how Maya Angelou succeeds in reaching out, touching others, and offering hope and confidence in times of humiliation and despair.

The poem begins energetically, speaking to an unnamed person (or persons):

> You may write me down in history
> With your bitter, twisted lies,
> You may trod me in the very dirt
> But still, like dust, I'll rise.

After asking several bitter questions: "Does my sassiness upset you?" (second stanza);"Did you want to see me broken? / Bowed head and lowered eyes?" (fourth stanza); and "Does my haughtiness offend you?" (fifth stanza), the speaker exclaims:

> You may shoot me with your words,
> You may cut me with your eyes,
> You may kill me with your hatefulness,
> But still, like air, I'll rise.

By applying repetitive rhetorical questions, the poet increases tension and strain, and by using the repetitious phrase "I rise," she emphasizes her courageous stance. She describes in her own characteristic spare manner her response to the past:

> Out of the huts of history's shame
> I rise
> Up from a past that's rooted in pain
> I rise
> I'm a black ocean, leaping and wide,
> Welling and swelling I bear in the tide.

Leaving behind nights of terror and fear
I rise
Into a daybreak that's wondrously clear
I rise
Bringing the gifts that my ancestors gave,
I am the dream and the hope of the slave.
I rise
I rise
I rise.

Maya Angelou is not a poet of hopelessness, but rather, the opposite. In the face of despair, she finds and absorbs inner forces that nourish her strength and sustain her courage. Maya Angelou states in one of her many fascinating interviews that she considers courage the most important of all virtues. She says: "Without that virtue you can't practice any other virtue with consistency."

Maya Angelou certainly doesn't lack courage, in her life or in her work. ❈

Critical Views on
"Still I Rise"

[This extract is taken from Robert B. Stepto's review of
Maya Angelou's third volume of poetry *And Still I Rise*.
Here he explores the poetic and visual rhythms of the
poem.]

And Still I Rise is Angelou's third volume of verse, and most of its
thirty-two poems are as slight as those which dominated the pages
of the first two books. Stanzas such as this one,

> In every town and village,
> In every city square,
> In crowded places
> I search the faces
> Hoping to find
> Someone to care.

or the following,

> Then you rose into my life,
> Like a promised sunrise.
> Brightening my days with the light in your eyes.
> I've never been so strong,
> Now I'm where I belong.

cannot but make lesser-known talents grieve all the more about how
this thin stuff finds its way to the rosters of a major New York house
while their stronger, more inventive lines seem to be relegated to
low-budget (or no-budget) journals and presses. On the other hand,
a good Angelou poem has what we call "possibilities." One soon dis-
covers that she is on her surest ground when she "borrows" various
folk idioms and forms and thereby buttresses her poems by evoking
aspects of a culture's written and unwritten heritage. "One More
Round," for example, gains most of its energy from "work songs"
and "protest songs" that have come before. In this eight-stanza
poem, the even-number stanzas constitute a refrain—obviously, a
"work song" refrain:

> One more round
> And let's heave it down.

One more round
And let's heave it down.

At the heart of the odd-number stanzas are variations upon the familiar "protest" couplet "But before I'll be a slave / I'll be buried in my grave," such as the following: "I was born to work up to my grave / But I was not born / To be a slave." The idea of somehow binding "work" and "protest" forms to create new art is absolutely first rate, but the mere alternation of "work" and "protest" stanzas does not, in this instance, carry the idea very far.

Other poems, such as "Willie," cover familiar ground previously charted by Sterling Brown, Langston Hughes, and Gwendolyn Brooks. Indeed, Angelou's Willie, despite his rare powers and essences ("When the sun rises / I am time. / When the children sing / I am the Rhyme"), approaches becoming memorable only when he is placed in that pantheon where Brooks's Satin-Legs Smith and Brown's Sportin' Beasly are already seated. Similarly, "Through the Inner City to the Suburbs," "Lady Luncheon Club," and "Momma Welfare Roll" bear strong resemblances to several poems of Brooks's pre-Black Aesthetic period in *Annie Allen* and *The Bean-Eaters*.

Up to a point, "Still I Rise," Angelou's title poem, reminds us of Brown's famous "Strong Men," and it is the discovery of that point which helps us define Angelou's particular presence and success in contemporary letters and, if we may say so, in publishing. The poetic and visual rhythms created by the repetition of "Still I Rise" and its variants clearly revoice that of Brown's "strong men . . . strong men gittin' stronger." But the "I" of Angelou's refrain is obviously female and, in this instance, a woman forthright about the sexual nuances of personal and social struggle:

Does my sexiness upset you?
Does it come as a surprise
That I dance like I've got diamonds
At the meeting of my thighs?

Needless to say, the woman "rising" from these lines is largely unaccounted for in the earlier verse of men and women poets alike. Most certainly, this "phenomenal woman," as she terms herself in another poem, is not likely to appear, except perhaps in a negative way, in the feminist verse of our time. Where she *does* appear is in Angelou's own marvelous autobiographies, *I Know Why The Caged Bird Sings* and *Gather Together in My Name*. In short, Angelou's poems are often woefully thin as poems but they nevertheless work their way into contemporary literary history. In their celebration of a particularly defined "phenomenal woman," they serve as ancillary, supporting texts for Angelou's more adeptly rendered self-portraits, and even guide the reader to (or back to) the autobiographies. With this achieved, Angelou's "phenomenal woman," as persona *and* self-portrait, assumes a posture in our literature that would not be available if she were the product of Angelou's prose or verse alone.

> —Robert B. Stepto, "The Phenomenal Woman and the Severed Daughter (Maya Angelou, Audre Lorde)," *Parnassus: Poetry in Review* 8, no. 1 (Fall–Winter 1979): pp. 313–15.

LYMAN B. HAGEN ON "STILL I RISE" AND THE BLACK SPIRITUAL "RISE AND SHINE"

[Lyman B. Hagen is the author of the book *Heart of a Woman, Mind of a Writer, and Soul of a Poet: A Critical Analysis of the Writings of Maya Angelou.* In this extract Hagen states that Angelou speaks for her gender and race in this poem.]

In this category is Angelou's favorite poem and theme, "Still I Rise," the same title as that of a play she wrote in 1976. The title, Angelou says, refers "to the indominable spirit of the black people." She often quotes this poem in interviews and includes it in public readings. The poem follows Angelou's customary fashion of incremental repetition, and catalogues injustices.

In spite of adversity, dire conditions and circumstances; in site of racial epithets, scorn, and hostility, Angelou expresses unshakeable faith that one will overcome; one will triumph; one will Rise! The lines remind us of the black spiritual "Rise and Shine" as well as other religious hymns that express hope: "Oh, rise and shine, and give God the glory, glory! / Rise and shine, and give God the glory, glory!" In "Our Grandmothers" Angelou voices a similar sentiment contained in another dearly loved spiritual: "Like a tree, down by the riverside, I shall not be moved."

The "I" in "Still I Rise" is designated female by Angelou herself as she numbers this poem as one of the four about women in *Phenomenal Woman*. She speaks not only for herself but also for her gender and race. This extension of self occurs in Angelou's autobiographies and protest poetry. It is in keeping with a traditional practice of black writers to personalize their common racial experiences. Moreover, Angelou implies that the black race will not just endure, but that in the words of Sondra O'Neale, "will triumph with a will of collective consciousness that Western experience cannot extinguish. Angelou's most militant poems are contained in the second section of her first volume of poetry, "Just Before the World Ends." They have "more bite—the anguished and often sardonic expression of a black in a white dominated world," Chad Walsh observes. In her moving address "To a Freedom Fighter," Angelou again as a spokesperson for all blacks acknowledges a debt owed to those who fought earlier civil rights battles. They did more than survive; they endured all indignities for the maintenance of their race.

—Lyman B. Hagen, *Heart of a Woman, Mind of a Writer, and Soul of a Poet* (Lanham, Md.: University Press of America, 1997): pp. 127–29.

Works by
Maya Angelou

AUTOBIOGRAPHIES

I Know Why the Caged Bird Sings. 1970.

Gather Together in My Name. 1974.

Singin' and Swingin' and Gettin' Merry Like Christmas. 1976.

The Heart of a Woman. 1981.

All God's Children Need Traveling Shoes. 1986.

PERSONAL ESSAYS

Wouldn't Take Nothing for My Journey Now. 1993.

Even the Stars Look Lonesome. 1997.

CHILDREN'S BOOKS

Life Doesn't Frighten Me. 1993.

My Painted House, My Friendly Chicken and Me. 1994.

Kofi and His Magic. 1996.

POETRY

Just Give Me a Cool Drink of Water 'Fore I Diiie. 1971.

Oh Pray My Wings Are Gonna Fit Me Well. 1975.

And Still I Rise. 1978.

Shaker, Why Don't You Sing. 1983.

Now Sheba Sings the Song. 1987.

I Shall Not Be Moved. 1990.

On the Pulse of Morning. 1993.

The Complete Collected Poems of Maya Angelou. 1994

Phenomenal Woman: Four Poems for Women. 1995.

A Brave and Startling Truth. 1995.

PLAYS

Cabaret for Freedom. 1960.

The Least of These. 1966.

Getting' Up Stayed on My Mind. 1967.

Ajax. 1974.

And Still I Rise. 1976.

Moon on a Rainbow Shawl. 1988.

SCREENPLAYS

Georgia, Georgia. 1972.

All Day Long. 1974.

Works About
Maya Angelou

Avant, John Alfred. Review of *Just Give Me a Cool Drink of Water 'Fore I Diiie*, by Maya Angelou. *Library Journal* 96 (1971): 3329.

Bethel, Lorraine. "Maya." *Equal Times* 20 (November 1978): 14–16.

Bloom, Lynn Z. "Maya Angelou." *Dictionary of Literary Biography*, vol. 38. Detroit, Mich.: Gale, 1985, 3–12.

Blundell, Joyce Boyarin. Review of *And Still I Rise* by Maya Angelou. *Library Journal* 103 (1978): 1640.

———. Review of *Shaker, Why Don't You Sing* by Maya Angelou. *Library Journal* 108, No. 7 (1983): 746, 748.

Chevalier, Tracy, ed. *Contemporary Poets,* 5th Edition. Chicago: St. James Press, 1991.

Cosgrave, Mary Silva. Review of *And Still I Rise* by Maya Angelou. *Horn Book Magazine* 55, No. 1 (1979): 97.

———. Review of *Oh Pray My Wings Are Gonna Fit Me Well* by Maya Angelou. *Horn Book Magazine* 52 (1976): 78.

———. Review of *Shaker, Why Don't You Sing* by Maya Angelou. *Horn Book Magazine* 59, No. 3 (1983): 336.

Cotter, James Finn. Review of *Oh Pray My Wings Are Gonna Fit Me Well* by Maya Angelou, *The Women and The Men* by Nikki Giovanni, and *The Peacock Poems* by Shirley Williams. *America* 134, No. 2 (1976): 103–4.

Crockett, Sandra. "Poetic Angelou Can Sing, Cut a Ring." *Baltimore Sun* 9 September 1997: E1, 8.

Elliot, Jeffrey M. ed. *Conversations with Maya Angelou.* Jackson: University Press of Mississippi, 1989.

Essick, Kathy M. *The Poetry of Maya Angelou: A Study of the Blues Matrix as Force and Code.* Indiana, Penn.: Indiana University of Pennsylvania, 1994.

Evans, Mari, ed. *Black Women Writers (1950–1980): A Critical Evaluation.* Garden City, N.Y.: Anchor Press, 1984.

Felton, Keith. "Womanflight on the Wings of Words." *Los Angeles Times* 28 December 1975: 70–71.

Fulghum, Robert. "Home Truths and Homilies." *Washington Post Book World* 19 September 1993: p. 4.

Gates, Henry Louis, Jr. *Reading Black, Reading Feminist: A Critical Anthology.* New York: Meridian, 1990.

_____. "The Blackness of Blackness: A Critique of the Sign of the Signifying Monkey." In *Black Literature and Literary Theory.* New York: Methuen, 1984, 285–321.

Gates, Henry Louis, Jr. and Nellie Y. McKay, eds. *The Norton Anthology of African American Literature.* New York: Norton, 1997.

Georgudaki, Ekaterini. *Race, Gender, and Class Perspectives in the Works of Maya Angelou, Gwendolyn Brooks, Rita Dove, Nikki Giovanni, and Audre Lorde.* Thessaloniki, Greece: Aristotle University of Thessaloniki, 1991.

Gilbert, Sandra M. "A Platoon of Poets." *Poetry* 128 (1976): 290–299.

Goldberg, Doris. "Poetry of Angelou." *The Blade* 5 November 1978: G10.

Goodman, G., Jr. "Maya Angelou's Lonely Black Outlook." *New York Times* 24 March 1972: 28.

Gottlieb, Annie. "Growing Up and the Serious Business of Survival." *New York Times Book Review* 16 June 1974: 16, 20.

Hagen, Lyman B. *Heart of a Woman, Mind of a Writer, and Soul of a Poet: A Critical Analysis of the Writings of Maya Angelou.* Lanham, Md.: University Press of America, 1997.

Harris, Kathryn Gibbs. Review of *Oh Pray My Wings Are Gonna Fit Me Well* by Maya Angelou. *Library Journal* 100, No. 17 (1975): 1829.

Howe, Michele. "Angelou's Poetry Builds Bridges Between Peoples." *Star–Ledger* (Newark, N.J.) 3 June 1990: C4.

King, Sarah, E. *Maya Angelou: Greeting the Morning.* Brookfield, Conn.: Millbrooke Press, 1994.

Liddy, Martha. Review of *Just Give Me a Cool Drink of Water 'Fore I Diiie* by Maya Angelou. *Library Journal* 96 (1971): 3916.

Lippmann, Ellen. Review of *And Still I Rise* by Maya Angelou. *School Library Journal* 25, No. 3 (November 1978): 108.

Lupton, Mary Jane. *Maya Angelou: A Critical Companion.* Westport, Conn.: Greenwood Press, 1998.

Magill, Frank N., ed. *Masterpieces of African-American Literature*. New York: HarperCollins, 1992.

Megan-Wallace, Joanne. "Simone de Beauvoir and Maya Angelou: Birds of Feather." *Simone de Beauvoir Studies* 6 (1986): 49–55.

Metzger, Linda et al., eds. Black Writers: *A Selection of Sketches from Contemporary Authors*. Detroit, Mich.: Gale Research, 1989.

Moyers, Bill. "Portraits of Greatness." PBS Home Video, Pacific Arts, 1982.

Neubauer, Carol E. "Maya Angelou: Self and a Song of Freedom in the Southern Tradition." In Tonette Bond Inge, ed., *Southern Women Writers: The New Generation*. Tuscaloosa: University of Alabama Press, 1990.

Plimpton, George. "The Art of Fiction CXIX: Maya Angelou" *Paris Review* 32, No. 116 (1990): 145–67. Reprinted in "Maya Angelou with George Plimpton." *Contemporary Literary Criticism* 77 (1994): 14–21.

Ramsey, R. Pricilla. "Transcendence: The Poetry of Maya Angelou." *A Current Bibliography of African Affairs* 17, No. 2 (1984–85): 139–53.

Readings on Maya Angelou. San Diego: Greenhaven, 1997.

Review of *And Still I Rise!* by Maya Angelou. *Black Scholar* 8, No. 1 (September 1976): 50–51.

Review of *And Still I Rise!* by Maya Angelou. *Library Journal* 103 (1978): 1640.

Review of *Just Give Me a Cool Drink of Water 'Fore I Diiie* by Maya Angelou. *Choice* 9, No. 2 (1972): 210.

Review of *Oh Pray My Wings Are Gonna Fit Me Well* by Maya Angelou. *Booklist* 72, No. 4 (1975): 279.

Review of *Oh Pray My Wings Are Gonna Fit Me Well* by Maya Angelou. *Choice* 12, No. 11 (1976): 1439.

Rochman, Hazel. Review of *I Shall Not Be Moved* by Maya Angelou. *Booklist* 86, No. 18 (1990): 1773

Shelton, Austin, ed. *The African Assertion: A Critical Anthology of African Literature*. New York: Odyssey, 1968.

Stepto, Robert B. "The Phenomenal Women and the Severed Daughter (Maya Angelou, Audre Lorde)." *Parnassus: Poetry in Review* 8, No.1 (Fall–Winter 1979): 312–20.

Showalter, Elaine, ed. *Modern American Women Writers.* New York: Charles Scribners, 1991.

Sylvester, William. "Maya Angelou." In *Contemporary Poets.* Chicago: St. James Press, 1985.

Tate, Claudia. *Black Women Writers at Work.* New York: Continuum, 1983, pp. 1–11.

Tawake, Sandra Kiser. "Multi-Ethnic Literature in the Classroom: Whose Standards?" *World Englishes: Journal of English as an International and Intranational Language* 10, No. 3 (Winter 1991): 335–40.

Wall, Cheryl. "Maya Angelou." In Janet Todd, ed., *Women Writers Talking.* New York: Holmes & Meier, 1983, 59–67.

Index of
Themes and Ideas